NO ONE CAN SEE THE WORLD I LIVE IN

sean::adrian::brijbasi

Published simultaneously in the United States and
Great Britain in 2021
by Pretend Genius
Copyright © Sean::Adrian::Brijbasi

This book is copyright under the Berne Convention
No reproduction without permission
All rights reserved

ISBN: 978-0-9995277-0-2

other books by Sean::Adrian::Brijbasi

One Note Symphonies
for Emma

Still Life in Motion
*for those who play
Marius and Andréus*

The Unknowed Things
for Julius

The Dictionary of Coincidences, Volume i
for Emma

S{E}AN?
for EM{M}A+

E{M}MA+ the ghost orchids
for Emma

darling two hearts
for E{M}MA+ the ghost orchids

Stories for Nadira
*for Adrian, Andréus, Elijah, Helena, Julius, Marius,
Nadira*

Play Championship World-Class
Tennis with Bjorn McEnroe
*for Adrian, Andréus, Elijah, Helena, Julius, Marius,
Nadira*

The World That Destroyed the World
for Adrian, Andréus, Elijah, Helena, Julius, Marius, Nadira

The Book of Lashonda
for Adrian, Andréus, Elijah, Helena, Julius, Marius, Nadira

ENTROPALACE
for my brother Troy

for

the

only

one

contents

Chapter 1 — 1
strategies for survival — 1
looking paths — 3
alpha particle — 5
matters of the utmost importance — 8
also imagined as — 11
pretending beyond sleep — 14
the unrelenting impermanence of things that matter, seen and unseen — 17
the tender epidermal layer — 19
cotyledon — 21
a serene and beautiful order of one — 23

Chapter 2 — 27
her hair was black — 27
the day maria bought her green dress — 30
Go. — 34
interspatial — 37
what do I have to think about to be happy — 40
superficial touching: study 3 — 42
minimum unassembled describable moment blocks — 45
the futuristic blueprint — 48
the start of the understanding of the presence of youth — 51
to know sorrow is to know every feeling — 54

Chapter 3 — 57
a tale to tell your melancholy mother — 57
the breezes of good feelings and others — 59
this kind of freedom (peripheral) — 62
submerged stones — 65
red jasmine flowers — 67
the off-key to happiness — 69
a fast-growing and evergreen laurel — 72
in the midst of happy times — 74
nobility, dignity, a serene inner beauty — 76
a flag of the triumphant — 79

Chapter 4 — 83
as it is — 83
the flowers of the trees, then the wildflowers — 85

3 seconds before the end — 87
visual remnants of a deep sub-conscious psychology and
the everyday reflections of the human struggle — 89
popliteal fossa — 91
a welcoming gesture to venture forth — 93
one of the living — 96
random sleep movements — 98
the sensations of possibility — 100
see life — 102

Chapter 1

strategies for survival

On days when Maria had nothing to do, she took a taxi to the airport and sat in the international arrival hall (with whatever book she was reading) and waited for no one in particular. She told herself many times she wasn't feeling what she was feeling, as if she were telling someone else, someone she knew only in passing, and who asked her one day "out of the blue", why she or he observed a sudden anxiety come over her when another person left the room—a departure which must have broken a deep and hidden connection to the departed and affected Maria in such a way as to turn her into a different person right before their eyes.

The question was always asked in this way—"why (she or he) observed"—to leave space (in Maria's mind and in the world *ex tempore*) for doubt about whether the observed anxiety was real or not. Or whether the observed anxiety was simply a product of projection. Maybe it was the observer who became disconnected. Maybe it was the observer who felt a sudden anxiety.

But in Maria's mind the observer never failed to convince her, after brief but intense arguments, that it was she (Maria) who became disconnected and that if she wanted to survive the disconnection she should place herself—not just mentally but physically, her whole body and all of its hidden parts—in a circumstance that provided the possibility of making her feel the opposite of departure—arrival—and so she sat with her book in the airport's international arrival hall, waiting for someone to arrive (and perhaps return) from somewhere far away.

She did this several times a week for many months until one day a woman walked through the automatic doors from the customs area and entered the arrival hall, carrying only a small backpack, looking lost in the music in her headphones, and who was greeted by no one.

looking paths

Maria followed the woman. First, to one of the small shops in the airport that sold snacks and beverages, where she (the woman) bought a bottle of water. Maria was also thirstiest after the plane landed, especially during the ordeal of finding her bag on the baggage belt. She thought perhaps she and the woman had more in common. She noticed the woman's shoes were comfortable the way she liked her shoes. But were those basic commonalities enough to start and continue a conversation?

"I like your shoes."

"Thank you."

It could end abruptly. So, Maria waited before she approached the woman. She followed her through the airport to, what was now, the exit through which Maria entered earlier. This exiting made Maria wonder if there was someone waiting outside for the woman. Perhaps this was a trip the woman had taken many times and whoever waited for her understood the disorder of the crowded arrival hall. Perhaps the woman and whoever waited for her had worked out their arrival routine over time until it was now at its most efficient.

But as Maria followed the woman it became clear to her there was no one waiting. The woman stopped at the bus stop and stood apart from the small group of people waiting for the bus. Maria also stopped and stood closer to the woman than to the small group of people. She wanted the woman to know that she too was separate though not the same. She too stood apart from the group but at a different distance, a different angle, and with a different lean of her body.

While the woman looked at the group from where she stood, Maria looked away from them, so the paths of their looking intersected. Maria calculated the location of the intersection and followed it first downwards to see eight blades of grass growing through the concrete, made brighter green by the afternoon sun (a hidden connection—of which there were many—that would last until winter); and then upwards to see the sky, the sun, and the clouds, moving slowly, though she could also see the clouds as not moving at all. But mostly she watched the space that occupied the intersection of their looking, watched to see if the air in the space moved in some way, vibrated, or varied its hue so that it was noticeable to the person who knew where to look and what to look for.

Sometimes the location of the intersection changed but Maria was always aware of the change, however slight, and recalculated the location several times before the bus arrived (twenty-three minutes later), before the looking paths that resulted in the intersections of their looking disappeared, before she found herself sitting next to the woman on the bus, a natural sitting that might have occurred even if Maria did not have an unbearable desire to sit next to her, as if she were simply getting on a bus and sitting on the seat closest to the exit, like she had done so many times before.

alpha particle

Maria dismissed the looking paths as ephemeral. She always did. She wanted things, objects, situations, entities, and most of all her feelings—

especially those related to her comportment—to be timeless. As useful and stimulating as looking paths were to gauge the dynamic of a situation, they were not timeless. After all, how could they be when they could change without warning, sometimes unknown to the observer, and when Maria was unable to control her own looking paths? She also obsessed about looking paths and their intersections to the point that she would forget everything else, including her comportment, and as she argued many times to anyone who would listen: something that can be obsessed about to the point of forgetting everything else simply *cannot* (emphasis hers) be timeless.

She thought she showed timeless courage by sitting next to the woman on the bus even though she also thought perhaps the arrangement happened by chance without the need for any timeless courage from her at all. She was aware, however, from recent experience that when someone gets what they want, they can never be sure—through their action or inaction—they didn't have something to do with it.

She calculated that she and the woman would have sat next to each other eight-hundred times out of a thousand based on their relative position and bearing during the outdoor circumstance they found themselves in immediately prior to getting onto the bus—during *and* in. Still, there was the possibility she would have to be timelessly courageous two-hundred times out of a thousand. Could she be?

It was the question that stayed in her mind during the bus ride; the question that caromed from one side of her head to the other with every bump of the bus's big tires and even when there weren't any bumps. There was another question that stayed in her mind during the bus ride also: how would she begin a conversation with the woman?

This question did not carom. While the courage question bounced all around her head like an alpha particle bouncing off the walls of an almost-empty room (with no windows or doors), the conversation question was like an alpha particle that hovered perfectly still right in the center. Sometimes it glowed.

matters of the utmost importance

The woman had already read the book Maria was reading (ENTROPALACE—"A shockingly concise demonstration of nonlocal entanglement and a masterpiece of the small books genre."). If Maria had known the woman had already read the book (or disentangled it) then she could have simply taken the book out of her bag and set it on her lap with the cover face up.

The woman would have recognized the cover—the bathtub in the palace of Minos—on the longer than usual bus ride and said: "I've read that book". It would have been the start of their conversation. But how could Maria have known? There were no clues, no indication in the woman's facial expressions or gestures, no list of books she had already read pinned to her shirt.

After all, such a list would be impractical to wear unless one only considered 1) the last book one read, 2) the book one is currently reading, and 3) the next book one will read (if known). Such a list was possible, conveying enough information (three "data points") to allow one reader (not an observer—as recognition and understanding of the words made one a reader) to infer a pattern about the other reader, and could be pinned anywhere on the reader's person—a shirt, a pants pocket (front or back), or even the side of a shoe.

Additional information could be added to the list, depending on the size of the letters and the sprawl of the reader's writing, though not much, and perhaps all the better to not ruin the aesthetics (and therefore the attraction) of the pinned list with clutter if at any moment a gentle breeze lifted the paper the list was written on to change the angle of observation (as the breeze lifting the paper made the list unreadable).

All angles must be considered Maria would say to the woman and smile "knowingly" (in the appropriate context), though she also understood the "abutting" of those words—*all angles must be considered*—to be more of a conversational decree strangely compelled by the uncertainty of first contact and not a reasonable archetype for everyday living and, one could assert, not a reasonable archetype for *second* contact.

Maria imagined (as she always did about people who sat next to her) that the woman was involved in matters of the utmost importance. So different from how she lived and the activities her life was centered around—waking (or walking?), doing unimportant things, sleeping. And yet she always had hope that one day, even if it was the day before the last day of her life, she too would be involved in matters, or at least one matter, of the utmost importance, and so she should not despair even when she admitted to herself (and there were many times, sometimes out loud)—half-asleep on her bed looking at clouds through her bedroom window, alone in a building stairwell, or as she sat quietly in the living room of a dimly lit apartment sipping her drink and watching friends talk—there was no hope at all.

also imagined as

Maria didn't know the woman was arriving and returning. There was the possibility she was only arriving. She carried a small backpack—light enough to place on her lap without touching Maria's lap, even as the g-forces of the bus turning at various points of its route (at the Avenue of Children, around the circle at Hanami Park) moved the bodies of the passengers in such a way as to instigate a sudden and collective straining of the essential muscles—refined and unrefined—to keep them from colliding against one another. Certainly (?), there were the unexpected touchings of shoulders—despite the expected g-forces—but nothing any reasonable person would have deemed (at the time) *extra-ordinaire*.

At the first major turn, the road curved right, which could have resulted in the woman's backpack moving onto Maria's lap and (Maria hoped) one or two items tumbling out—maybe a pen the woman had used to write in her journal or maybe the hallowed journal itself with scribbles and drawings made by the woman that imparted her ways of living (a.i.a. her ways of being in the world) to any stranger who might find it if she had dropped it on one of her walks to the grocery store. But the backpack held firm on the woman's lap as did the contents within.

At the second major turn, the road curved left, which provided the opportunity for Maria to relax her body and "by accident" touch the woman's shoulder (and arm area) with her own. This would have given Maria the chance to apologize and begin the conversation she thought would be the start of (something). She saw herself apologizing and immediately easing into the conversation with all the aplomb of a seasoned raconteur, as if the apology and every word that followed were as natural as the letters of the alphabet following one another in their predetermined order or like honey flowing through a cup of the bitter tea it sweetened. But she instinctively tensed her muscles at the turn and the moment was lost as the road straightened and the bus continued a straight path for several miles. She rued the straight path while on it but it gave her more time to devise her more nuanced plan.

One major turn remained—a curve to the right, before the bus entered the city where all turns (those designed on purpose or formed by accident) were minor turns and would occur too slowly to create the g-forces needed for Maria's more nuanced plan to succeed. Maria knew of this turn. She had taken this bus ride many times: during sunny weather, during light rain, and on holidays during heavier rain.

She would place her leg closer to the woman's leg at the very start of the turn and, as the turn progressed, move her leg closer still. Then at the apex of the turn—the succulent vertex of the parabolic curve—"transport" her leg the half-foot needed to touch the woman's leg with her own to make it seem as if the woman's leg had touched hers instead. The woman would turn to Maria to apologize which would serve as the impetus for any following conversation.

As a way of figuring out what she would say to the woman after she accepted her apology Maria used a strategy she had never used before: she first thought about things she would not say and added their opposites (if the opposites were clear) to her mental list of "things to talk about with the woman". Unclear opposites were discarded or added to another mental list (for now). Maria thought this strategy, despite the risk of never having tried it, would lead her to the right words and if not the right words, then at least the topics of conversations that were the most interesting and possibly—if the unknown conditions she had always hoped would come to her aid, came to her aid for once—the most scintillating.

pretending beyond sleep

Sometimes when Maria rode the bus, she saw (what she thought were) tiny rain drops striking the window glass. Rain drops never appeared to fall gently to her, even when she was younger and her mother or father read stories to her about the soft clouds, the tender grass, and the gentle drops of rain falling on the eyelashes of children as if the tears they cried for bruising a knee or being slapped on the head by a school teacher streamed up instead of down their little child-faces. And then, of course, one teardrop getting trapped by the hair follicles of their little child-eyelashes.

Rain drops always looked like they struck to Maria. And this striking action was more pronounced by the time a rain drop hit an object directly in its path. She imagined either an explosion that destroyed both the drop and the object or a devastating penetration that only destroyed the object—a hollowed out carcass left in the wake of precise rain drop destruction.

When Maria was most unsure about whether she was seeing tiny drops striking the window glass but wanted to be sure, she focused on one spot of the glass, like a crepuscular opportunity predator, pretending to be asleep, but who was only half-asleep. She waited for a drop to land in her hunting range area and then instead of viciously attacking with every claw and tooth at her disposal, she kindly observed.

If she saw nothing, she moved her search. Sometimes she widened the search area to include more window glass (all the while pretending to be asleep with the slimmest viewing channel for her pupils, and sometimes a single pupil, like the viewing channel of a jaguar suffering both hunger and exhaustion—so slim in fact that none of those tiny drops she tried to kindly observe would have been able to slip into her pupil or the surrounding pupil area, even if she turned her face straight up to the sky whence they came).

Sometimes when she pretended to sleep, she also pretended to dream, which didn't make anyone think she was dreaming but did make everyone think she was sleeping because she was pretending beyond sleep. Sometimes afterwards she thought maybe she did dream—about the lonely jaguar roaming her surrounding pupil area then stopping to stand over the pupil and drink as if it were drinking from a jungle pond; or about having a conversation with someone she loved who was no longer alive, although the conversation was always mumbled and unclear; or about seeing the reflection of people in the window glass who smiled only with their mouths, the way people who suffer smile when friends tell them to smile and take their photographs. Sometimes her pretend dreams made her cry in real life, although she wanted to tell someone, maybe the woman sitting next to her, that every time she was dreaming about one thing, she was crying about something else.

the unrelenting impermanence of things that matter, seen and unseen

There were no tiny drops of rain to observe. Instead, the sun was bright and shined through the window glass of the bus and onto the floor between the rows of seats like the sun shining over the city of Maria's memories. She looked down on her city as if she were a god and saw them all but wondered about her city's edges—the land near the borders that darkened until they reached darkness. She thought her city should be large and larger still. Why was it so small when she had lived so long and gone so far?

She felt that even as a god she was powerless to change her memories. She could only change the telling of them—make them more expansive, attach new memories to old spaces and old memories to new spaces—so the sun shining on the narrow floor between the two rows of seats on a bus in which she sat next to a woman she wanted to speak to, might shine on the whole bus and, if her mind did not break apart, shine on the space around the bus and then beyond that space and further still. Or perhaps the sun would shine too brightly. In the darkest spaces. Not to uncover new or hidden memories but to obliterate them with light. To make them and the darkness in which they existed unseeable.

Maria's attention turned away from her shining city on the bus floor when the woman leaned her head against the window and closed her eyes. Maria felt the woman's movement in the seat and heard something tap against the window glass. She pretended to look through the window—at the clouds, at the trees, at the birds flying between the clouds and the trees, but she stared at the woman's face: her cheeks, her nose, her mouth, her eyelids, which sometimes twitched as if she were dreaming. Or perhaps they twitched because she was troubled by the brightness of the sun. The same sun that shined on Maria's city, that uncovered new and hidden memories, that obliterated with light until unseeable.

the tender epidermal layer

The bus was still miles away from the 6 Cities, from the final curve that would create the g-forces necessary for Maria to carry out her plan. She closed her eyes also and listened to the sounds around her, absorbed them through her skin (so they streamed just beneath her tender epidermal layer but no further)—the sound of people talking and whatever words she could make out but mostly the sound of the bus, the engine and the wheels, which made her think of artificial water moving through steel pipes, an epiphany that burst like a soap bubble, the scent of which lingered in the air around her for seconds after the bubble's bursting—seconds in which she was so moved by the unexpected fragrance of the clean and fresh air that she secretly declared her love for most of the people who lived in the world. A declaration that was still sincere for several minutes after it was made.

She pondered the sincerity of her declaration. Did she really love most of the people who lived in the world? She thought "I am breathing and living (or loving?) now". The thought made her body tingle and while the feeling felt real, or so she thought, it was more of an animal feeling. The sincerity of her declaration of love surprised her because it carried her towards the feeling of love. And she thought for a moment that she did, in fact, feel real human love. She had been uncertain about whether she still had real human feelings. She thought maybe she only had the memory of them and that her real human feelings transmuted a long time ago. Maybe after the very first time she felt them—the first time she felt sadness or anger, love or hate, was real, but any time after the first time she felt them, they were copies. Maria liked the idea of copies because she thought real human feelings made human interaction almost impossible.

cotyledon

On days when Maria didn't take the bus to the airport, she sometimes lingered at the music conservatory near her apartment where she might sit in on an orchestra or choral rehearsal. Free music was the right of every human being she thought. Even her, who alleged she didn't hear well because of an insect. If she could just see the instruments— the brass, wood, and silver-colored objects coupled with human mouths and hands, then she could indulge in the sounds she could hear and imagine the sounds she couldn't hear (or thought she couldn't).

She could hear perfectly well but an insect did enter her ear on a day she picnicked with her mother and affected her hearing for days during which time she thought perhaps the insect might have given her extraordinary powers by deforming her inner ear as it burrowed into the vestibular or tympanic duct (or other areas of the ear) when it tried to (and finally did) free itself. Maybe the power to hear music better or the power of perfect pitch (or both and other ear powers) so she could hear and know the notes warbled by a house wren or the chord(s) played by the bottom of a metal gate scraping the concrete when a child (or someone older) pulled the gate open. Or just come to appreciate the polyphony of sounds in the normal world around her which up until then she had never thought about, never really noticed, and couldn't say convincingly she appreciated.

She stayed in her bedroom for days after the insect entered her ear, as if she were inside a seed, waiting for the moment when the powers took hold of her, like sun and rain, and she could break through the outer boundary and perhaps one day, she imagined, blossom to her full magnificence. Instead, she seemed to hear less. She thought the insect diminished her hearing, after all, even as the sound of artificial water flowing as it might, along a plastic river bed, an earthy river bed, or through a steel pipe (the sound she heard on the bus), became clearer and clearer to her all the time.

When she didn't linger at the conservatory or take the bus to the airport, she walked around the 6

Cities and visited parks and shops. Her favorite park was the Flower Viewing Garden where the insect entered her ear as she picnicked with her mother. Her favorite shop was the fan shop owned by the old lady from Ishikawa prefecture, to whom she had once asked a question about a fan. Sometimes she sat down at a cafe' or brasserie. She preferred sitting outside. On colder days or days of light rain, when all the tables and chairs had been moved inside, she would ask if a table and chair could be moved outside (if it was no trouble). She did the same things other people did when she wasn't taking a taxi to the airport. Other people also took a taxi to the airport so, it could be said, she was always doing something other people did.

a serene and beautiful order of one

The bus neared the curve before it entered the city. Maria's last chance to attempt her more nuanced plan. It was her only plan. She didn't think of a second plan and she didn't think about the idea of a second plan until it was too late. When the curve came, the g-forces were so strong that Maria was unable to "transport" her leg to touch the woman's leg. The bus driver had taken the turn faster than usual and Maria didn't understand why. He had never taken the turn so fast before. Years later she would remember having the thought (why so fast?) whenever she traveled on a bus. It had become part of her bus-riding and, occasionally, bus-catching routine.

Maybe it was all for the best (she reasoned with herself), as the bus passed under the archway that welcomed travelers to the city, because she never did think of anything to say to the woman. She thought of different words but not a single cohesive sentence. Words alone (pinecone, cowhand, rhododendron) without context weren't enough.

In a few short miles, the bus would stop at the 6 Cities Central Station—renamed for the city—where all the passengers would alight and go their separate ways, as if they were atoms released from temporary confinement, flying further and further apart from one another until each was alone—something that resembled the entropy of the universe, but was in Maria's mind, if not *quod in posterum*, a serene and beautiful order of one.

After the curve, the bus stopped at a traffic light. The first stop in the city. Maria saw the woman lift her head from the window (using her peripheral vision). It was a vision Maria used only by chance now, unable to use it voluntarily as she did when she was a child and when, it could be argued, the accessibility she had to all the different types of human vision (peripheral, rudimentary, transverse and many others) seemed to make her perspective of the world—like the perspective of all children—a singular work of art. The unexpected peripheral vision could be an indication that her body and its senses were bringing all its powers to bear, even its weakest, on solving this one problem.

The bus stopped at the station. The passengers alighted. Maria needed to catch the next train to World A or she would have to wait for hours. She exited the bus before the woman, who walked behind her. There was no time to do anything. No backward vision to use, no opportune moment to turn around, no excuse to pause to let the woman walk past her. There was no action Maria could take. In retrospect she thought maybe she could have paused or maybe taken some other action but she had steeled her mind to the situation—she never spared herself—and walked resolutely to the train platform to wait for the train.

Chapter 2

her hair was black

Maria found an unoccupied cabin on the train to World A. She sat down, leaned her head against the window, and closed her eyes. She had about an hour to go before she arrived at her next destination and the tension she felt sitting next to the woman during the short trip from the airport to the train station had worn her out.

It felt as if her muscles exhaled and breathed normally again, easing into a state of relaxation while her mind remained ever vigilant: ever vigilant to the arrival of strangers (and people she knew but whose names she couldn't remember), ever vigilant to a change in the atmospheric pressure, ever vigilant to a lurching of the train before it transitioned to the smooth and comfortable ride advertised by the train company on posters displayed around the 6 Cities: "The Smoothest Ride Ever or Your Money Back".

The ride was smooth after all she decided. Her body rarely shook on the many train rides she had taken and she never once felt the need to ask for her money back. She supposed she could have asked but she couldn't think of how the asking would be justified. The ride was really smooth—the smoothest ever.

She opened her eyes and lifted her head from the window. She reached into her bag (without looking) and took out the book she had been reading (ENTROPALACE—"A book within a book but not of a book."). If she had taken this very same action on the bus, she and the woman would have probably had the conversation she was hoping for when she first saw the woman at the airport. Now there was no one around her but she was content. She crossed her legs and balanced the book on her lap—didn't touch it with her hands—and when she moved to make herself more comfortable and the book felt as if it would fall, she adjusted her body to steady it again.

She remembered the two men who sat across from each other on a train ride she took the week before. They argued about the rules of a game she was vaguely familiar with while she looked out the window quietly, watching the trees and any animals or people she saw as the train passed by them. Her book was still in her bag and she felt that reaching for it, even without looking, would draw unwanted attention to herself.

She tried to think about something that would make her feel undisturbed in their presence. She couldn't think of anything at the time but since then she had come up with a short list of things to think about when she wanted to feel undisturbed in the presence of others:

1. two flowers in the same vase in a dark room—one in full bloom and one dead

2. her stolen kite "aloft" on a grey, cloudy day, flying above houses in the distance—she could see it from her apartment balcony

There were five things to think about on her list at the beginning of the week but three of them no longer worked. She tried each of them during different circumstances in which she found herself disturbed in the presence of others. One of them

(#4) failed her on the same day it was put on the list and two others (#1—at the time, and #5) weakened until they were unreliable after only a few days. She was down to two things to think about to feel undisturbed in the presence of others and she thought maybe she only needed two. So far, they worked every time because after thinking about either for only a few minutes, she felt undisturbed.

The train started its short journey without a hint of a lurch—smooth—and she leaned her head against the window again, though this time, she kept her eyes opened. She wore a sleeveless green cotton dress that came to her knees. Her hair was black.

the day maria bought her green dress

The day Maria bought her green dress was a holiday in the 6 Cities. It had rained earlier in the morning and there was chatter—she heard it on her walk to the Flower Viewing Garden—that the celebrations might be postponed or cancelled due to the unexpected bad weather. All the months of planning by adults and children, by the old lady from Ishikawa prefecture with help from teenagers who attended the 6 Cities High School (renamed for the city), all the days and weeks of work required to celebrate for the twelve hours from noon to midnight (the food from Maria's favorite brasserie, the festive banners, the street plays, the musical bands, and later that night the fireworks) might be wasted, it could be argued, because of rain.

Maria wanted to be around the celebration. She liked light happiness even if she didn't feel it herself. She liked to see it. In the same way she liked to see light sadness. She considered herself "a tactician of the light feelings of human beings", if only because she liked the way the words fit together. It must be or mean something if they came to her out of nowhere as if from different directions in the air and joined together (so well—she thought).

When she saw someone smile or look up to the sky and sigh in frustration (or express other light feelings), she assigned the words to herself (a tactician of the light feelings of human beings) without using the words "I" and "am" or—proving her self-control—the tempting contraction. In her mind, it was understood—as it would be in the mind of anyone else who was a tactician of the light feelings of human beings because it was possible the words and the order in which they came did not come to her alone among billions.

She would start from her apartment a few minutes before noon and walk from neighborhood to neighborhood—from World A to the Flower Viewing Garden to the Avenue of Children to Hanami Park, through the closed roads at the center of the city, and then, taking a different path, return to her apartment from where she would watch the fireworks from her balcony. All through her walk she would be considered "pleasant to see" by anyone who noticed her and truly "beautiful in the sun" by those who had not seen her in some time but saw her standing on the other side of the road or sitting on the stairs of one of the buildings in the 6 Cities designed in the neoclassical style.

The light rain in the morning gave way to the sun by noon and Maria did as she planned except on her return to her apartment later that evening, she saw a green dress in the window of a shop she had never visited before. She could see from the sidewalk that the dress would fit her—she was always good at sizing up clothing, more so blouses and loose-fitting tops than dresses but she was still very good with dresses. She bought the dress without trying it on and continued on her way home where she changed into the dress and lay on her bed with her legs hanging over the edge. The hem of the dress came above her knees.

Later that night she stood in her living room, in front of the sliding glass door that opened to the apartment balcony and watched her reflection, watched how the dress fit her body, watched the fireworks light up the dark sky over the 6 Cities, and when it was all over, sat down on her sofa and crossed her legs, as she might if she were sitting in the window seat in the cabin of a train.

Go.

Maria heard voices approach the train cabin and took a quick glance toward the door. Her body tensed up in anticipation of someone entering (two flowers in the same vase in a dark room—one in full bloom and one dead). She thought that if someone did have to enter (of all places, this place) then let it be a woman. The hem of her dress disturbed her skin—raised the tiniest hairs on her knees and thighs—as she fidgeted in her seat. She uncrossed her legs and adjusted her posture to sit with the soles of her comfortable shoes flat on the train's metallic floor. The vibrations from the train's locomotion traveled through her body and she thought that at sub-atomic levels, and perhaps even higher atomic levels, it was difficult for the train that provided the smoothest ride ever (at human levels) to maintain its smoothness.

The voices grew nearer. She opened her book. She listened, tried to make out what she was hearing, but she couldn't understand. The people spoke clearly enough but in a language she didn't know. She scanned random words on the first page of her book—she had lost her place—without being aware of what she was reading (*"birds flying feathers calm"*). She expected the cabin door to open at any second but minutes passed and no one entered.

Her body relaxed. She closed her book and crossed her legs. As she leaned down to put her book into her bag, her peripheral vision—one of her weakest powers, but a power which seemed to have become more reliable than ever—activated as it had done on the bus. She caught a glimpse of someone in the corner of her eye and moved her looking path towards the cabin door. She held her book—aloft and slightly open—over the opening of her bag without placing it inside. She saw a woman pass by. Not all of her but enough of her—the wavy black hair, the shoulder, the back—to make her believe it was the same woman she followed through the airport and sat next to on the bus. The train conductor followed behind her.

Maria fidgeted in her seat (again). She uncrossed her legs (again). She opened her book (again) and it was as if all the words and letters in her book, including the table of contents, the dedication ("for my brother Troy"), and the page numbers had fallen into her bag during the few seconds she watched the woman walk by, leaving the pages blank except for one page (of unknown number) upon which remained a single word: Go.

She picked up her bag and opened the cabin door. She walked behind the conductor. The woman walked in front of him and then sat down in a seat by a window, squeezing past the legs of two people to do so. Maria sat down in an aisle seat in the row behind. She watched the woman's face between the seats—her profile and sometimes (almost) her whole face if a sound attracted the woman's attention so that she turned her head to look. Was this the face of the voice Maria heard? She plumbed the depths of her recent memory and remembered many relevant details—a language she didn't understand, the touch of her dress's hem, birds flying feathers calm—but as for the (now) mysterious voice, she remembered neither the tone nor the timbre.

interspatial

The human body is beautiful Maria thought as she looked at the woman's face. Sometimes the opposite thought came to her but she preferred this one. The thought started at the very top of the woman's head and, despite Maria not being able to see all of the woman's body, worked its way down to her feet. Every part of the woman's body, seen and unseen, including the interspaces between her toes, enhanced the thought or was enhanced by the thought (or both concurrently) as if the thought and the different parts of her body were two dancers taking turns to lead. For example, the thought enhanced the woman's eyes, lips, and arms while the thought was enhanced by her legs, stomach, and ears.

There was no chance of speaking to the woman under the circumstances. Maria couldn't see herself reaching between the seats to tap the woman's shoulder to say (What? The human body is beautiful?) above the chatter of people and the mechanical noises of the train. She would have to speak loudly and Maria never spoke loudly. Her voice volume was somewhere between a whisper and what would be considered the normal voice volume of a polite person.

She imagined herself and the woman floating in their seats above the other passengers and through the top of the train so that instead of sitting inside the train they sat above it, undisturbed by any wind, rain, or snow as if they were protected within an orb of golden light (each in her own) that cushioned them in the present while the future, with its platinum buildings and artificial radiance, passed them by. And where, instead of hearing the chatter of people and the mechanical noises of the train below, they barely heard the lightest breeze (also the present) penetrating the vast and silent air around them (also the future). The woman would turn to look at Maria and Maria at her and they would know that when the train reached its destination and returned them to the land of many people, they would find each other and speak at last.

Maria wondered why she didn't think of the idea while they were on the bus. Perhaps it was because the bus didn't always travel in a straight line (a path she once rued). At first, she imagined that none of the other passengers noticed her and the woman disappearing through the top of the train but thought the disappearance would be more meaningful—make her happier somehow—if one person noticed: a man sitting behind them, reading a book, and who happened to look up when he heard the click of the train conductor's ticket punch and saw what was happening to Maria and the woman (right behind the train conductor's back) and then saw them again together, after all the passengers had alighted, speaking in a distant and quiet corner of the train station.

Later, he would try to explain what he saw to his wife (who waited for him outside) while she drove him home. He would be happy to see her, tell her he loved her, and hold her hand all the way to the driveway of their house.

what do I have to think about to be happy

The woman put her headphones over her ears and disappeared, if not literally through the top of the train, then figuratively, into the music she was listening to. Even if Maria wanted to tap the woman's shoulder to get her attention there might be no way of reaching her because music could make one's body numb to trivial interactions (for example, superficial touching) while the mind plumbed ever deeper into the labyrinthine melodies of a favorite tune. She thought of music as both an 'out there' and an 'in here'—an entanglement in both a figurative and literal sense, an *unendlichbeideSinnekeit*—an infinite-both-senses-ness—which could be unraveled as an entanglement of its own.

If the past was something that grew out from and extended behind Maria (from the top of her head to her heels) and the present a miniscule self-contained capillary in her left shoulder that drew blood from the outside world to distribute only within itself (and to no other parts of her body) then what was all that remained of her? Maria wanted headphones also. It could have been only the two of them on the train, both "in here" and "out there".

Perhaps a keen observer would have noticed—the man thinking about his wife—which would have made Maria happy in the same way that being observed as they disappeared through the top of the train would have made her happy. She wanted to be happy in that moment, even if slightly less happy (without headphones and observer) than she could have been (with) and thought "what do I have to think about to be happy". For her, the thought wasn't a question as there was no answer she could provide. Not that she didn't know of an answer. There simply was no answer for her to know.

The train stopped to let on more passengers. Maria looked through the window and mistook a leaf hanging on the limb of a nearby tree for a man (with a hat on his head) bending over in a field to pull something from the ground. The sun, high above him, was blocked from her view by the top of the same tree and it occurred to her:

1) the sun did not cause the light shining on the earth,

2) the timing of the sun's "rising" and the fading of darkness on the earth was a coincidence, and

3) the people who studied the sun (and, in time, everyone) would see this after the sun had died

The train started moving again. The train conductor made his way further to the front of the train. Maria saw him through the doors that led from one compartment to the next. Soon, he would move to other compartments further away until she could no longer see him.

superficial touching: study 3

The train glided forward, parallel to Old 6 Cities Avenue, once a main thoroughfare of the 6 Cities but now a back road that shadowed the train tracks "across the way" for several miles before it ended in the approximate vicinity of the old 6 Cities city limits. Maria looked through the window and saw two women on a motorcycle, moving along the avenue, faster than the train. The wind blew the long hair from beneath the black helmet of the woman riding the motorcycle onto the shoulder of the woman sitting behind her, who turned her head to look towards the train so that light, possibly from the sun, reflected off the top of her helmet and into the circle-shaped hearts of Maria's eyes—her exquisite pupils.

Then the motorcycle slowed and turned into the city between the structures of a perpendicular road—as if turning from a thin line on the human hand into the throbbing pulse itself—disappearing from Maria's view as the train continued along its track (a.i.a. the vein of a barren yet graceful arm, the skin hairs like wispy flora on the surrounding landscape). It was a moment that would engrave itself in the granite part of Maria's memories, if not forever, for a long time.

She could make what she wanted of the engraved moment—mold the granite like clay—as there were many accounts that existed within it. As many accounts as there were observers, though she could experience only one. An account, like all accounts, which was something more than an interpretation but something less than reality. Just as she would never know the leaf hanging from the tree was not a man bending over to pull something from the ground (she would try to guess what it was and even visit the field for clues), she would also never know the woman on the back of the motorcycle turned her head to look away from the train and not look at it because looking at the train would have made her dizzy. Maria's memories, and her life, were and was, shaped as much by truths as they were by untruths—more than she knew—like the memories and life of everyone she shared them with.

She could imagine sharing this memory with the woman she wanted to talk to—ask her if she saw the two women on the motorcycle (since she was sitting by the window) and tell her that the woman on the back of the motorcycle turned to look at the train at the same moment she (Maria) looked at her as if they sensed each other like two exhausted human animals lost (but hiding) in a forest. Maria would know what to say and would be so happy to say it that, without thinking, she wouldn't give the woman time to respond.

"Do you believe in such things?"

"Does it happen to you?"

"It happens to me."

"It's happening to me right now."

minimum unassembled describable moment blocks

The motorcycle and the two women disappeared into the city. Maria didn't know where they were going. She thought they would ride through the 6 Cities streets and stop at her favorite brasserie—park, remove their gloves, pull off their helmets, and unzip their jackets. They would leave their helmets on the motorcycle—the woman in front would hang hers on one of the handlebars while the woman who rode on the back would place hers on the seat. They would walk to an outdoor table (under the green but faded awning) and drape their jackets over the backs of their chairs, sit down to look out onto the street, and drink from the brasserie's flower-patterned tea cups while the sun's light shined on their legs.

Maria could see through the doors to the other train compartments. Maybe as far as two compartments. She had no experience of herself being in them—she never sat in a train compartment lower than compartment four. She imagined them to be the same, as the sun might imagine its light near the earth (or other planets and interstellar objects) to be the same, though it also had no experience of itself being in those places.

The man sitting next to Maria leaned forward and put his forehead against the back of the seat in front of him. Maybe he wasn't feeling well or maybe he was in a contemplative state but he blocked Maria's view so she could no longer see the woman. She used the time to keep thinking (calmly—she knew the woman was still there): she and the sun were the same, after all, whether either was associated (by external studies) with the light or the being emitted from their respective bodies into near or distant spaces. The sun was there, rain or shine. And so (she thought) was she.

The man leaned back in his seat again so that Maria could see the woman again. She had removed her headphones from her ears and let them hang around her neck. Her skin glowed as Maria had never seen it glow before and she wondered what music had filled the woman's ears and, in turn, her brain to make her feel as if her body was immersed in a different, more vivid life? A different, more vivid life that was part of her same life (observably so).

But Maria would have been mistaken and she might have raised the corner of her mouth slightly at the mistake if she were made aware of it because there was no cause and effect between the music and the woman's skin. Maria had simply used her active mind to sequence the minimum unassembled describable moment blocks around her to give them meaning and allure—to match the sky—because what was life if not meaningful and alluring?

The man leaned forward (again) and blocked Maria's view (again) but she still saw the top of the woman's head, saw the headphones go up, saw the woman's hands adjust the pads around her ears and, after only a few seconds, saw how the woman's skin glowed beneath her hair. There were three and half songs to go before the train reached its destination. Three and a half songs of glowing.

the futuristic blueprint

If Maria made a futuristic blueprint of her position and the woman's position on the train for the women on the motorcycle to discover years later and study—when futuristic blueprints were considered out of fashion—they (the women on the motorcycle) would have seen, that although Maria and the woman sat diagonally behind one another on the train, they (Maria and the woman) would have looked like they sat next to each other—if the women on the motorcycle viewed the futuristic blueprint from behind.

And if the women on the motorcycle were as clever as Maria thought they were (she would have left no instructions) and viewed the futuristic blueprint from all angles, including the oft-unobserved side angle, they would have seen that

Maria and the woman looked like they sat directly behind one another and not diagonally, as if they were riding a motorcycle also.

Maria had learned to ride motorcycles with small engines when she was a teenager, so she was cautious about the futuristic blueprint, especially the side angle. She could have been in front, after all. And although she thought the futuristic blueprint was an accurate relic of the times, she also thought that observing the futuristic blueprint from all angles made it inaccurate (though accurate enough), and merely connotative in the way two dolls made of mud and straw, painted with the dye of insect blood, and decorated with the leftover cloth of a woman's shawl, were connotative.

Maria played with dolls when she was a girl but not enough to justify them as gifts for her birthday. Her parents gave her a doll twice and after the second time, when they realized she had placed the second doll next to the first doll without ever picking either one up again, gave her only books which she used as dolls instead, staging them in scenes throughout her room, depending on the illustration or title on the cover of the books.

Eventually she would read her books and rearrange them according to the stories therein and then put the staged books away on her shelf after she read them all, until she received more books—stage, read, rearrange, and shelf. She already knew where she would put the book she was currently reading (ENTROPALACE—"water for those who aren't thirsty, food for those who aren't hungry") with the photograph of a bathtub on its cover and drawings of birds without eyes on the pages inside.

Upon discovery of the futuristic blueprint, the women on the motorcycle might have dropped it as a useless bauble, but it would have been at that very moment, when the futuristic blueprint contacted the ground from the height of a woman's waist, that they would have seen one woman glowing and one woman not glowing because one woman was deep in the solitude of life while the other was a little deeper. And they would have thought that life, like those dolls at the time they were made could be ugly or beautiful, but survival like those dolls at the time they were found, whether ugly or beautiful, was always beautiful. Then they might have picked up the futuristic blueprint again and studied it a little longer.

the start of the understanding of the presence of youth

"Hi Maria."

"Hi Dad."

"How are you?"

"Fine."

"How was your first day at school?"

"Good. My teacher said I'm a good speller."

"You are a good speller. Did she ask you to spell any words?"

"Yeah, a lot of words."

"And you got them all right?"

"I didn't get pneumana right."

"You mean pneumania?"

"Yeah I didn't get it right."

"That's a tricky one."

"Yeah that's what Ms. Pnear said."

"Your teacher's name is Ms. Near?"

"Yeah but she said I came close."

"Do you know how to spell it now?"

"Yeah. P, n, e, u, m, a, n, i, a. She said the p is silent."

"Yeah, it is silent."

"I don't understand."

Maria couldn't tell if the woman was younger than her. She thought they were the same age, though it didn't matter. Maria only felt the absence of youth, not the presence of it. She didn't know what the presence of youth meant. She wasn't old enough yet and understanding one (the absence) didn't mean understanding the other (the presence). She remembered the first time she went to the grocery store by herself. She dressed as if it were a special occasion, like her mother used to dress, when her family went shopping once a week on Sunday mornings in lieu of church. She would tell Maria to wear her nice dress—already laid out on her bed for her to change into after breakfast. Maria wondered how the dress suddenly appeared on her bed and one Sunday paid close attention to her mother while they were sitting at the table. Her mother got up to go to the sink and then slipped out of the kitchen. It became a game they played every week. And every week Maria would eat her breakfast in anticipation of walking into her bedroom as if she were walking into the secret room of a museum to see a dress, occasionally a new dress, framed by the contours of her bed. It was the first memory she had related to the start of her understanding of the presence of youth. More (silent) memories would come.

Maria thought the woman was young and beautiful, which in her mind meant innocent and true. Maybe she remembered going to the grocery store by herself for the first time also. Maybe she was a good speller. The woman slid her headphones off her ears (mid-song) and onto her neck. She looked out the window. The train slowed until it stopped and then a commotion as people got up from their seats to walk down the narrow aisle and out. The woman didn't stand up until everyone left. Maria did the same. They were alone in the train compartment. The woman turned her head but didn't look at Maria. Maria stood up, walked past the row the woman was sitting in, to the exit door, and finally the two steps down onto the train platform. She felt the breeze from the sea on her skin.

to know sorrow is to know every feeling

Maria worried about bad things happening to people she loved. She didn't love the woman but she was starting to worry that something bad might happen to her. She imagined the woman standing defiantly on the train tracks as the train ran over her body, the engineer having seen her too late to stop the train's substantial locomotion in time. Or waking up to see the woman's head against the train window, her skin pale and no-longer-soft, having suffered a sickness due to an unexpected change in elevation. Or while walking along the train platform, knocked over by school kids running to catch another train, causing her head to hit the hard concrete, her life slipping away as people gathered around her, some of whom might have felt guilty for thinking she looked "beautiful in the sun" as the sun reflected in pupils that could no longer take in its light. Maria would have been too far away to hear the tumult.

World A was miles behind her and she wasn't sure where she was going. She hadn't planned on taking the train so far. The idea of speaking to the woman mixed with the air and noises around her (the cold milieu of reality) no longer seemed possible. It was as if the train ride were another life of contained possibility she could no longer live in the uncontained air.

She heard the announcement to begin boarding the ferry, destination: 6 Cities Island (renamed for the city). She had never been there before. She knew that few people lived on the island though it did have its own grocery store and post office, and even a tower constructed for housing the bell that rang three times a day between sunrise and sunset—the 6 Cities Island Bell. The first ringing could be heard across the sea in the quiet of morning.

Maria wondered why she imagined the woman standing defiantly on the train tracks and not meekly or sadly. Maybe she thought the woman was stronger than the train. But what about those other thoughts she had about bad things happening to the woman? A sickness due to a change in elevation (not defiant) or hitting her head on the concrete (also not defiant); then she thought the woman might have fought her sickness to the end (defiant) or fell because of another sickness, which she fought to the end (also defiant) and she was satisfied that the arithmetic of her thoughts about bad things happening to the woman resolved to defiant.

She boarded the ferry and leaned against the railing—her left foot on the bottom rail, her arms on the top—and looked out to the water as the crossing got underway. She saw small boats, saw birds flying in the sky, saw children swimming near the shore of the island from where it appeared the sun travelled in a blaze along the surface of the sea (and who knew to what depths?) to shimmer along the contours of her body.

Chapter 3

a tale to tell your melancholy mother

The ferry cut across the 6 Cities Sea current like a naginata blade dragged along hot concrete into uncut grass. Maria's mother told her the sea never froze, even on the coldest days, so warm was the sea water during winter. During summer, the sea water was cool and refreshing, especially on the hottest days. As the air temperature rose, the sea temperature fell. And vice versa.

Maria's mother also told her—she told her three tidbits about the sea—the 6 Cities Sea was the warmest place to be during a 6 Cities winter, though not necessarily the coolest during a 6 Cities summer, and (with a tinge of melancholy in her voice) "if birds could fly under water and flowers grow between the sea surface and the sea's gloomy bottom then that was exactly what would have happened while soft but driving snow strafed the evading-but-unescaping waves above".

On some days, the temperature of the sea surface and the temperature of the air were the same though no one could predict on which days the singular harmonization might occur, despite the sublime intelligence of the air, sea, and earth scientists who wrote and/or spoke on the subject throughout the years. Maria's mother was an air scientist (of sublime intelligence) and predicted the harmonization most likely occurred, if in fact it ever did occur, between four and five in the morning during the months of October, June, and August. This was the third tidbit Maria's mother told her about the sea so Maria felt she was prepared to make the sea crossing for the first time—a little knowledge about the sea, after all, surely gave her an advantage over random sea crossers and perhaps the sea itself.

She looked around the ferry for other sea crossers but saw no one else. She realized she was alone and, except for the ferry driver (who didn't factor into the count), the only person crossing the sea unless another person was hiding somewhere on board. She mentally searched all the places a person could hide on the ferry (there were only a few) considering body shape, hair length, and foot size, and determined such a hiding was unlikely if not unachievable. After her search she concluded she was alone and crossing the sea by herself—a solitary sea crosser on a slow-moving ferry (though not with sadness).

This was a tale she could tell her mother, whose sublime intelligence would allow her to hide her melancholy when thinking about the sea so that her smile might look sincere as her daughter told her the tale of her crossing—a pleasant crossing of air and sea, and earth in the distance.

the breezes of good feelings and others

With no one else on board the ferry, Maria was free to roam about. She moved along the railing like the arrowhead on the second hand of a rectangular clock, keeping irregular time, stopping now and then to look down to the water to see if she might spy indications of sea life. But the wake and the foam caused by the ferry's hull hid the sea life beneath the chaos of white bubbles ("water-turmoil") or most likely scared the sea life deeper and deeper towards the sea's gloomy bottom (gloomy for Maria but not for the life beneath the sea).

She walked all the way around the ferry, stopping and spying, though spying nothing until she returned to the spot from where she started (more than a minute later), and from where she looked out just a little further away from the ferry and spied a shadow in the water—"sea life" she thought and considered the shadow enough evidence of such life to yell out the two words to her mother later that day in what was, for the *känsliga öron* of both women, an above average voice volume.

The breeze felt good on her skin. She closed her eyes and thought no matter how the day started and the disappointment of not talking to the woman on the bus or the train that this breeze (its multiple directional angles, skin-perfect temperature, and velocity) would have made whatever life forms in the alternate mise-en-scène of life forms that lived in her soft and manicured brows think they were living in a blossoming garden with an assortment of breezes (sea and otherwise) that affected them—sometimes almost deeply—in different ways each day (or hour or minute) and today affected them with the breezes of good feelings about the world around them.

This was the "feelings" Maria absorbed through her skin but could only partially feel (and not surprisingly around the area of her brows). She thought that if she were an arrowhead on the second hand of a clock turned towards the center of the clock and not away from it—and then nothing as the "feelings", though partial, overtook her so she couldn't finish the thought at that moment and she realized, later in the day when she returned to the thought to finish it, ever. She closed her eyes and listened to the water, listened to the birds she could hear, listened to the faint voices of the children playing on the shore across the sea.

this kind of freedom (peripheral)

As Maria looked out to the trees on 6 Cities Island her peripheral vision activated—it seemed stronger than ever—and she saw to her right (while also looking at the trees) a small sailboat drifting (sail aloft) and bobbing (rudder up), allowed by its sea captain to drift and bob in whatever direction the sea current was taking it; a sea captain viewed by sea captains and shipmasters of higher rank observing from various shores, as both strong for being able to "let go" and weak for not being "in control".

Maria was a strong sea captain who thought she was being tempted into thinking about freedom as the sailboat drifted from the sea into the canals of her thoughts—the wind, the sail, the open sea; but this wasn't her kind of freedom and she wouldn't be thinking about "it" (or any other kind of freedom) in the middle of the day and with so much exposure in all directions.

This kind of freedom (peripheral) might lead to drowning. She didn't like being in the water—in the same way she didn't like picnics in the woods or picnics in wide open fields—as water might enter one or both of her elegant ears and fill up her slight body (of so little weight compared to the weight of the world or when she was on land, the square footage of earth starting beneath her feet and extending through the earth's molten core) to sink her to the sea's gloomy bottom.

The sailboat drifted out of her peripheral vision as she continued to look at the trees, not falling for the second temptation to turn her gaze in the direction of the sailboat's absence. The voices of the children faded as the ferry got closer to the island—something else she couldn't have noticed if her ears were filled with water—and she saw they were no longer playing on the shore.

Sometimes when she sat on the park benches (mid-morning) in the 6 Cities parks, which she did often, she fell into a daze from not having slept well the night before and imagined she could get up and take two steps and walk through and over the trees in the park and then through and over the trees that lined the 6 Cities outskirts miles away (she would have to grow instantly).

Each step would be so gentle no one would notice her giant form above them and think (if they even reflected on it) that fast-moving clouds passed in front of the sun for a moment to offer them a brief respite on a hot day. On cloudy days no one would notice. And on rainy days people might feel dry for several seconds but not long enough to think something had gone awry.

Maria wasn't sure about the sea though—its depths in various locations and the length her beautiful legs would have to be to walk through and over the trees that grew from the bottom of the sea and then from the depths of the sea through and over the trees on the island itself. She was afraid of underestimating. The sailboat drifted into her peripheral vision again but there would be no third temptation. She let it drift in its location to her right, as it had drifted before she noticed it, but without letting it drift into the canals of her thoughts like it did minutes before.

submerged stones

The ferry was halfway to the 6 Cities Island. Maria thought she heard the island bell ringing and started counting the rings in her head. By three the count had moved from her head to her lips. She whispered counts four and five before the surroundings made it difficult to hear the ringing, then impossible. It wasn't a count she could start over, like counting submerged stones as she swam along the bottom of a river (in her bare feet) with a river-bottom map in one hand and nothing in the other.

She imagined the count all the way to twelve, thinking that along the way she would meet up with the ringing again (at nine) like two friends who had diverged in the woods and converged later at the river bank, to walk (and swim if they crossed) side by side as they had walked (and swam) before. But she didn't hear the ringing again and, in the short time it took for her to count from five to twelve, doubted she had heard it at all.

The speed of her doubt surprised her. Seven seconds before she would have told anyone who asked, "do you hear the bell ringing?" that she did hear the bell ringing. And years later she might have told someone else, true to how memory works though not true to the memory itself, that she had seen the bell ringing on her first visit to the island, an occurrence that would have surprised her (she would have described it as such) as she walked the upper outer island path along the cliffs from which she could look down to see the island houses, roads, and beaches.

The bell tower was down there somewhere also. She would have looked for it when she heard the fourth or fifth ring, like anyone who was visiting the island for the first time, while all those who lived there or visited many times continued doing what they were doing without distraction or disturbance. She thought if she had lived on the island, no matter how long, she would still stop what she was doing and look for the bell when it rang. Maybe not all the time—to stay connected to the island. But sometimes—to separate herself from it.

red jasmine flowers

The ferry stopped and Maria fell into the sea. She had taken a few steps back from the railing to sit down and felt water around her arms and over her head. She looked up and saw light diffused along the bottom of the sea's surface. She had plunged deeper than she would have expected after such a short fall. Above her, the ferry started toward the island again. She wouldn't have understood how it had gotten so far away so quickly.

The first memory she ever had (different from the first time she remembered) was of a time she lived by the sea. She remembered a desk and chair in a small room with a window. She remembered the wooden floors and the dust. She remembered hiding under the desk because there was space between the desk and the chair for her small body to fit, though she didn't remember why she was hiding. She remembered the distant sound of the sea.

It was a decaying memory—like a brightly painted scene on a piece of fabric that had been torn off from the whole and left under a dense hardcover biography to fade over time. She remembered it more brightly colored when she was younger—when the biography was thinner. Now the memory was gray and brown.

She didn't remember the broom in the corner, the blue and yellow rug, the photographs of clouds and birds her mother had taken, the single photograph of her mother descending the veranda stairs her father had taken. She didn't remember the red jasmine flowers outside the door always left opened at night to cool the room, the books stacked on the desk and the floor, the pen and inkwell always returned to the same place each evening.

She didn't remember standing on the small trash bin, emptied of its contents and turned upside down for her, to look through the window and watch the sea at night, the thousands of stars, the moon—

sometimes behind thin passing clouds—while her father scribbled on sheets of paper behind her.

All the bright colors had become gray and brown; the sea, the stars, and the moon had become the distant sound of the sea; and watching them at night through the window had become hiding beneath her father's desk. Maria's body had taken her as far as it could. The sea currents around her were too strong and she couldn't keep herself afloat. The ferry would travel back along the same path to return to the city but no one on board would have seen her.

the off-key to happiness

The current pulled Maria down. She had taken a deep breath and held enough air in her lungs to see a bird slice through the water beside her to catch a small fish between its beaks. She felt the water-turmoil on her face and slender arms, the reverberations of which reached her legs though she couldn't feel anything below her waist because of numbness.

The bird looked at her, its small black iris reflecting the image of her body descending deeper into the sea, and it appeared as if her body had descended into the bird itself, as if the bird had caught her soul (and the fish) and would fly back up to the surface and then further, to the upper limits of its celestial milieu (the troposphere), to give her soul one last glimpse of all earthly things, including the sea.

Maria held onto her bag thinking she could use it as a flotation device but she sank ever deeper into the sea's gloomy bottom. The book inside her bag (ENTROPALACE—"a small encyclopedia of bird life and a must read for those who occasionally read when they feel like it") weighed her down. She had closed her bag tight—used every available button and zipper—so there was no chance of it coming loose to release its denser contents into the surrounding water and perhaps save her life. If she had forgotten the book on the bus or on the train then she might have floated back up to the surface and taken another gulp of air as forgetting, like air, is an essential part of survival, if not happiness.

She wouldn't remember mentally saying goodbye to her mother (more forgetting) as her eyes closed but she would remember feeling two hands on her shoulders, the sea water in her mouth, and the grip of her wet green dress, cold and tight around the parts of her body unaffected by numbness. She opened her eyes and saw the sun beyond the jib of a small sailboat. The captain of the sailboat—the woman she followed from the airport onto the bus and from the bus onto the train—had pulled her from the sea.

Maria started to sing quietly. Her mouth was the only part of her body that worked and only for singing. She worried she was singing off-key but she sang so quietly that no one—in this case, the only one—would have been able to hear her. She thought no one could blame her for singing off-key if she were happy, and she didn't believe the woman, the only one, would mention it.

a fast-growing and evergreen laurel

Maria lay on her back on the sailboat's deck as if she were lying between two neatly trimmed hedges of a fast-growing and evergreen laurel. The motion of the sea-waves moved the blood inside her body and she felt her arms and legs again, felt the air on her face. She raised herself at her nimble waist and rested on her elbows. She saw a woman holding the sailboat's rudder behind the mainsail and the mast, her wet, black hair "gamboling in the breeze".

She couldn't see all of the woman's face, in the same way she couldn't see all of a person's body when she lay on the grass at the Flower Viewing Garden (on a warmer than usual Saturday) and looked through the neatly trimmed hedges—after hearing footsteps crunching the pebbles—to see who walked along the path on the other side. She might see the person's legs or if the person bent over to pick something up, an arm or a shoulder, and occasionally part of a face. But the entanglement of the hedge's bright green leaves and branches hid most of the person's body from her view.

And Maria would perspire. In the same way her skin was slightly wet above her lips on the sailboat (from the sea), it would be slightly wet on those warmer than usual Saturdays (from light perspiration) as she lay under the sun—a sheen of allure hidden from strangers who might consider her pleasant to see and acquaintances who had not seen her in some time but who would be reminded of how beautiful in the sun she was and always had been.

The woman steered the sailboat toward the island. Maria heard the children's voices again. They had boarded the ferry to cross the sea for the short passage from the island back to the 6 Cities—animated and excited because for them the end of a trip was as filled with possibility as the beginning. She saw part of the woman's face behind the mainsail and started to perspire lightly. Maria liked light perspiration. She thought light perspiration made her look more beautiful. Like raindrops on the laurel leaves after the rain.

in the midst of happy times

The woman sailed elegantly and Maria (thinking about elegance) finally had something meaningful to talk to the woman about. Once they reached the island, she would thank the woman for pulling her out of the volatile sea and saving her life. It was *the* elegant solution to the problem she struggled with on the bus and the train (though not on the ferry). She thought having your life saved by someone made for easy conversation—between the saved and the savior, the thankful and the thanked.

She lay back down on the sailboat's deck, flat on her back, and put her wet bag on her gentle stomach. Water dripped from the bag through her dress and onto her gentle stomach skin. She wouldn't talk to the woman until they reached the island because the wind and the sea were too noisy and she couldn't communicate with the nuance and texture she desired. Once on the island, however, she would speak to the woman using a combination of words in subtle tones she had never used until then. Maybe the woman would do the same.

Maria didn't want to plan her words. They would be unscripted and combined in a way never combined by any human being before; by any human being at the same time, while she was speaking them; and once forgotten, by any human being after, including her. No longer would she use the strategy of thinking about things to not say then add their opposites to her mental list of things to say. The strategy seemed passé now and made her chuckle, though without facial expressions.

And though she chuckled without facial expressions, she felt serious. Like she and the woman were two serious people living in serious times so that the memories they shared would feel like winter memories and not summer memories, because while summer memories were sometimes devastating (unexpected in the midst of happy times), winter memories were always serious.

The breeze and Maria's light perspiration cooled her brow under the mid-day sun which she could see high above the jib. She covered her eyes with her arm and secretly watched the woman through the curve of her inner elbow, who reached into her own bag to take out a sandwich (half a sandwich as she had eaten the other half on the plane). The woman took a small bite from one of the three corners of the bread. She held the sandwich with one hand while elegantly turning the sailboat's rudder with the other.

nobility, dignity, a serene inner beauty

While Maria lay on the sailboat she thought again about "if she were an arrowhead on the second hand of a clock turned towards the center of the clock and not away from it". The words came to her exactly as they had come to her on the ferry. If she had the thought earlier in the week as she strolled along one of the 6 Cities main boulevards, satisfied she was getting all that life had to offer her during her walk—good and pleasant air, some powers of observation, a few interesting thoughts, endurance for the distance of her walk—then she might have entertained such frivolity to a conclusion. But on the sailboat, as on the ferry, the thought crumbled as it was being formed. One could say the crumbling was an essential part of the thought's existence, which (poignantly) made the thought exist without end.

A few years ago, Maria saw a woman walking towards her on the Avenue of Children from some distance away. The woman saw her too. They looked at each other as they walked because staring didn't seem impolite from so far away. They continued smiling as they passed each other and quietly said hello. The smiling, like the looking, also started from far away and if anyone were observing Maria—perhaps sitting at an outdoor table at her favorite brasserie across from the fan shop owned by the old lady from Ishikawa prefecture—they wouldn't have been able to connect her smile to the woman walking towards her (or if observing the woman from the fan shop, connect the woman's smile to Maria).

Later that afternoon, in her apartment, Maria tried to recreate her gait and demeanor as she walked towards the woman. She walked towards herself in her hallway mirror in the same way, pretended to move her hair from her face in the same way, smiled in the same way. She wondered if she looked funny—maybe that's why the woman stared and smiled at her for so long. Or maybe the woman was drawn to her like she was drawn to the woman, saw something in Maria that she (Maria) brought into existence and nurtured—nobility, dignity, a serene inner beauty—that glowed through her skin and into the outside world on that day for those few minutes.

For most of the re-creation Maria walked in place, which did look funny, because there wasn't enough distance between herself and the mirror. She tried to remember the woman's smile, the woman's face, tried to remember deep into the woman's skin but she had already forgotten. She lay down on her sofa and started to fall asleep as a breeze drifted through her opened window (in the afternoon) and over her face which connected her to the feeling of that day and would connect her to the feeling years later whenever she lay down to fall asleep near an opened window (in the afternoon), whether a breeze drifted through it or not.

a flag of the triumphant

The woman walked past Maria, creating a breeze that mingled with the breeze created by the natural forces of the world (the sun, the sea, the earth's rotation, and the air pressure) around them. The breeze created by the woman made Maria think that to live in another world one must also live in this world. It was the inescapable truth of being (somewhere else). The woman threw a rope to the old man on the dock and stepped off the boat. They spoke as if they knew each other but Maria (who thought the old man dressed like a boy) didn't hear what they were saying.

When Maria was a teenager, she drew a picture of a rowboat and its reflection in the water(s) of the river that flowed near her mother's home. She didn't draw sails on the boat—the idea would have seemed alien (not of this world) to her—and yet there she was standing on a boat with sails. She lost the drawing when she moved to the 6 Cities. She thought it was her best drawing and tried several times to recreate it (from memory) but failed.

Over the years she feigned ambivalence about the drawing (when she imagined someone asking) but knew if she found it among her objects, she would like it as much as ever again, maybe more after missing it for so long. She never planned a search but looked as she picked up or put down an object—a honey jar, a winter boot, a paper clip. Sometimes when she looked, she expanded the area of her search but it was always *within the vicinity of*.

She had shown the drawing to people she no longer knew so there was no one left to talk to about the drawing, no one left to tell her how well she had colored the boat's reflection in the river or how the river captured the calm aftereffect of the storm that passed over the village earlier in the afternoon. In the future she would show her drawings to people she thought she would know for a long time, so that if she lost the drawings, she would have someone to talk to about them.

The woman disappeared on the other side of the boathouse and reemerged on a bicycle riding up the road to the places where people live. She stood up to pedal as the incline increased, perspiring lightly from the exertion. The breezes of the natural forces of the world tussled her hair. Her dress clung to the front of her legs and fluttered behind her like a flag of the triumphant.

Chapter 4

as it is

Maria found her own bicycle behind the boathouse. She placed her bag in the bicycle basket attached to the handle bars and started pedaling up the hill, perspiring lightly with each pedal, then half-pedal. She hadn't ridden a bicycle in a long time and her muscles were no longer accustomed to the bicycle-riding movements of her arms and legs. Less than half-way up the hill she dismounted and walked the bicycle the rest of the way. She saw the woman riding ahead of her and thought she would catch up once she reached the top.

The last time Maria rode a bicycle was in high school on an afternoon when no one was at home to drive her to tennis practice. She was new to the sport but the other players weren't very good and all it took for her to make the team was to read the book *Play Championship World-Class Tennis with Bjorn McEnroe* and practice her slice forehand and backhand in the parking lot against the school's auditorium wall. It was the first time she rode on a big road with so many cars because it took less time to get to the school and she didn't want to be late. The team was practicing high backhand volleys—a shot she only practiced in her mind and she was eager to practice the shot in real life.

She usually rode her bicycle on sidewalks and small roads on which few cars drove. She didn't tell her parents she rode on the big road because they would worry about what might have happened to her. She wondered if they thought about her death like she thought about theirs and she didn't want to add another possibility to the thought, even though she believed she had to think of all possibilities so that if anything happened to her parents, she would be prepared to go on living.

Maria imagined the moment during the bicycle ride when she and the woman would ride side-by-side. It would happen naturally, like the moon passing in front of the sun. The woman wouldn't slow down to let Maria catch her—she would be tired from riding up the hill while Maria was rested from walking. In terms of science Maria would conserve energy (a scientific law she learned from her mother) and she would use whatever last bit she conserved for faster pedaling when she reached the top.

She imagined that she and the woman would feel the strange power and sadness of being aware of another human being one was in harmony with as they rode side-by-side, quietly and without acknowledgement; an unstated harmony—to be part of a thing and to not speak of it, to not linger on its arrival or departure, and to hold the time of its existence, its essence, in one's consciousness, as it is, without reflection.

the flowers of the trees, then the wildflowers

Maria reached the top of the hill and mounted her bicycle. She pedaled at a normal speed—exerted no extra energy to catch the woman who rode ahead of her. She pedaled her bicycle calmly, passing houses along the road, beneath a Pau Rosa tree as pink flowers floated around her shoulders and legs, softer than rain.

In the tree, between a fork of two thick branches, a black cat with a small white patch on its chest sat and looked down on her as she rode by—happy with its own time and place, happy with Maria passing by to spend a fleeting (though timeless) moment with her. It existed like a bird flying in the sky or a turtle hiding in its shell or a wolf hunting with its pack, and all other animals people watch and pretend to be to learn how to become human.

The woman turned the corner and Maria sped up to make sure she didn't lose her. She considered her brief acceleration pardonable because she knew that in every life one must re-calibrate one's course to make sure the thing that turns the corner doesn't get away. When she saw the woman again on the road ahead, she resumed her normal pedaling speed.

She had pedaled out of reach of the falling pink flowers of the Pau Rosa tree, out of view of the black cat with a small white patch on its chest, but she had entered a new path lined by Laburnum trees of yellow flowers. Flowers which also fell slowly but even softer than the pink flowers of the Pau

Rosa tree, softer than the mist from the sea that cooled her face during the ferry crossing to the island.

As she pedaled, she felt perfect and powerful—like a porcelain vase appears on the outside, though on the inside there remains a little bit of old water and the dead petals of the wildflowers she might have picked from the fields around the village she lived in when she was young.

3 seconds before the end

From the road atop the 6 Cities Island, Maria saw the skyline of the 6 Cities across the 6 Cities Sea. She had come so far in the time she lived from the airport to the island and filled her little body with so much life that she thought if her life had to end right then and there on the bicycle beneath the falling flowers of the Laburnum tree, she would be able to convince herself within four or five seconds that she had taken enough life, wasn't shortchanged in any way, and bless life for offering her everything it could in the time she lived.

But there would have to be a warning. An inkling. A sense of something dire in the four or five seconds before the end because if it happened without warning (one or two seconds before the end) she might be confused, might not have enough time to think the thought, and therefore close the matter with life (her life), regardless of all the good and bad that happened to her—if not for practical reasons (because why would it matter?) then for aesthetic ones—on good terms.

But it did not end then and there on her bicycle beneath the falling flowers of the Laburnum tree or as she rode from beneath the tree's shade into the sunlight and onto a wider road with houses on both sides, outside of which people sat on their steps, ate island fruit, drank island drinks, and talked to each other when the mood suited them. She heard music and wondered if there was a holiday on the island not celebrated in the city. People waved to her and she waved back. People smiled at her and she smiled back. As if it were normal.

Maria would remember this passage. The angle from which the images of the people entered her eyes might even make her dream about them because they entered from the perfect height—slightly above eye-level—for retaining dream material (unknown to her) deep in her mind. She felt more encouraged than ever to have a conversation with the woman and to thank her for pulling her out of the sea. Afterwards they would talk to each other when the mood suited them. About anything. Part and see each other again.

visual remnants of a deep sub-conscious psychology and the everyday reflections of the human struggle

The speed at which the woman rode her bicycle slowed. Maria had conserved her energy on the climb up the hill and used her conserved energy to keep a faster pace after they reached the top. Maria would catch up to the woman by the middle of the next row of Hibiscus trees of purple, pink, and white flowers after which the pair would begin the long, straight ride (side-by-side) to the island's uninhabited region, rarely visited by locals during the summer heat because of the stealthy island insects. Maria had experience with insects. The insect in the park for example that might have entered her ear.

After they rode through the woodlands at the end of the road and into the opening on the other side where the swirling breezes kept the insects away, Maria and the woman would park their bicycles using the formal kickstands and sit near the edge of the cliff, look out to the sea, and talk about the long day from the airport to the island, about their journeys before they became aware of each other: Maria quiet in the taxi, keeping her bag on her lap although she thought about placing it on the seat next to her because of her dress, the taut but soft skin on the back of her thighs touching the vinyl seat; the woman eating half a sandwich, putting her headphones over her ears, leaning her head back, closing her eyes, only opening them when the airplane landed—visual remnants of a deep sub-conscious psychology and the everyday reflections of the human struggle.

When Maria finally caught up to the woman near the middle of the row of Hibiscus trees, they pedaled at the same pedaling rate, their legs turning in synchrony. As they moved along the road they pedaled faster and faster (influenced by each other) and smiled (uninfluenced by each other), then laughed (also uninfluenced by each other) in the way people laugh for no reason when they feel the wind on their face for a longer than usual time, though not too long. The woman turned to Maria and yelled: "we're going so fast!" to which Maria yelled: "we are!". They yelled because the wind made too much noise for them to hear each other using their normal voice volume.

popliteal fossa

Maria thought about how her voice sounded when she spoke normally (somewhere between a whisper and what would be considered the normal voice volume of a polite person) but this was a rare circumstance which required her and the woman to yell—though politely. It had been a long time since she had spoken to anyone while riding a bicycle. Perhaps it was the same for the woman.

She imagined what the woman's voice sounded like when she wasn't yelling. She thought she heard it in the train though she couldn't be sure because voices in a train—the way words sounded and were heard—reminded her of her dreams. She couldn't extrapolate from what she'd heard in the train to scientifically classify ("imagine correctly") the woman's pitch, rhythm, or pronunciation for later recall or recognition. Even the woman's yell in the island wind from the moment before offered no distinguishing or isolating features Maria could discern.

Soon, however, they would speak using their normal voice volumes and characteristics, including any disfluencies, as they might in the natural world. They would sit close enough together to communicate with nuance and sometimes let a simple gesture (unobserved from a distance) or the ebbing of a sentence, both content and volume combined with a downward casting of their eyes—the woman's of blue, Maria's of brown—to create something with their minds they could not find in the world around them, and imbue their shared space with meaning.

The Lapacho tree of pink and yellow flowers marked the entrance to the woodlands they would ride through to reach the clearing on the other side. The woman looked at Maria while Maria looked straight ahead to make sure nothing blocked their path.

"Let's go!" the woman yelled, speeding towards the thick tangle of trees.

"Let's go!" Maria yelled and forgetting herself, stood up to pedal and raced ahead.

From her stand-up riding position, with each downward pedal, her smooth popliteal fossa could be seen just beneath the hem of her dress.

a welcoming gesture to venture forth

Maria and the woman followed a path through the woodlands. They pedaled more slowly than when they were on the road because the trees in the dense overstory—the Custard Apple, the Wild

Cashew, the Lauraceae—blocked sunlight from reaching them and their eyes had not yet become accustomed to the darkness. Maria could no longer hear herself pedaling or the wheels of the bicycle turning, even though she felt the bicycle frame rattling on the uneven path beneath her. It was as if her living had become silent among the trees and she wondered if the woman's living had become silent too.

As she travelled further into the woodlands, she saw hummingbirds flying in and out of thin beams of sunlight that reached the dark understory. Sometimes two or three paused to drink nectar from the red flowers of the Heliconia. She saw butterflies and other insects taking off (from) and landing on tree trunks; ants marching along tree roots that bulged out of the warm earth. She saw palm tree leaves that looked like the fans at the fan shop owned by the old lady from Ishikawa prefecture, where fans with hummingbirds and butterflies painted on them decorated the shelves and the countertops from where she might pick up a fan and fan herself to cool her warm brow like the breeze moving through the trees cooled her warm brow as she mustered every bit of conserved energy to persevere.

As she neared the end of the path, sunlight revealed bird tracks on the dry earth that looked like the letters of an unfamiliar language. Maria couldn't decipher their meaning—didn't understand the words they formed—but took them to be the elements of a friendly message from the natural world. Perhaps a bittersweet good-bye (for the departing) or, if one entered the woodlands from the other side, a congenial hello (for the arriving), and a welcoming gesture to venture forth as birds scattered from the treetops in all directions. Maria was departing.

She saw the bright sky ahead, heard the uncontained sounds of the sea, and felt a boost of energy flow through her tired legs. As the path became smoother, she stood up to ride and pedaled faster than she had ever pedaled before. She pulled on the handlebars to lift the front wheel of her bicycle off the ground and raced into the sunlit clearing on one wheel. The woman pedaled faster behind her to keep up but continued riding on two wheels.

one of the living

Maria parked her bicycle using the formal kickstand while the woman placed her bicycle on its side (carefully)—didn't drop it (carelessly). They found a grassy patch among the stones on which they could sit and look out to the sea, to the 6 Cities across the sea and, if they so desired, observe askance the airplanes ascending and descending beyond the city from where their journey began.

Maria turned to look at the woman—looked at her so closely she saw the shadows cast by her eyelashes on the clear blue irises of her sad-and-happy eyes. She followed the woman's skin-line from her temple to her neck where it continued beneath the airy fabric of her dress, the shoulder seam lifted by the breeze now and then, to reveal the noble (hard yet soft) collarbone.

Maria believed she could explain to anyone—people might ask—how she and the woman were like two pieces of wood that had been set on fire and after burning slowly for a time, collapsed, and settled on themselves as they glowed and simmered, their smoke rising from the cliffs overlooking the sea to attract the attention (to "pause the life") of water-frolicking children, boating adults, or hard-working fisherpeople. The thought pleased her because fire only burned the living—spared the unliving—and she always felt deep in her being that she was one of the living. She had fire as proof if anyone doubted.

"Thank you for pulling me out of the sea", she said.

The woman turned to look at Maria (their looking paths collided) smiled and nodded once. Maria felt at that moment—the moment of the nod—that anything was possible, that a little girl might fall from the sky and into the sea, drift onto the shore near the 6 Cities, and make her way through the world to be happy.

random sleep movements

If it were dark instead of bright and Maria and the woman lay on the patch of grass among the stones in the clearing overlooking the sea, they would fall asleep and miss all the fragile happenings of the night around them—the single bloodflower near Maria's hip illuminated by moonlight, the deep green shell of a glorious bug navigating the rocky landscape towards the darker woodlands, or the flickering of a star, the light of which only reached the earth after it had been dead for millions of years.

Maria and the woman would be fragile too. Their bodies beside each other, though apart, as if placed there. But if by chance—due to random sleep movements—the fingers of the hand of one touched the shoulder or (more intimately) the fingers of the hand of the other, neither would be aware unless the touching conducted an electricity through their bodies to their brains and generated dreams, vivid and elusive, of the sky and the sea, of each other, and of the fragile world they lived in as it might appear to them if they looked down upon themselves as they slept.

Maria heard voices in the distance and stood up to look out to the sea. She saw the ferry and the children on the ferry pointing; heard them screaming. A single cloud moved in front of the sun and darkened the sea so that Maria couldn't make out what the children were pointing at in the cold, (now) dark waters. Not too long ago they would have been pointing at her as her body floated up from the water turmoil below.

She looked up to gauge how long it would take for the cloud to move away from the sun. It was a slow-moving cloud so it might take a few minutes. She thought about her mother (the air scientist) who had explained to her that clouds don't move the way humans move—that what she was seeing when she saw a cloud move was the result of water vapor condensing at different altitudes while the wind moved the water vapor in different directions.

Maria glanced at the woman (who lay on her back and closed her eyes) while she waited for the cloud and thought about what she should say next.

She had already thanked the woman for pulling her out of the sea so she believed it was time for a normal conversation—the kind of conversation other people have (which didn't involve thanking someone for pulling them out of the sea). Maybe she would tell the woman her name and ask her for her name though she thought that knowing each other's names would mean starting all over again—as if they were meeting for the first time—and bring about all the dangers such a primal encounter entailed.

the sensations of possibility

The woman opened her eyes and rested on her elbows. Maria heard the woman's body movement on the grass and turned to look at her. She looked at Maria. Under the darker sky they seemed like two dying sunflowers bending toward each other in a field of dying sunflowers—still imparting an eternal nobility as they aged, but their heads bowed, the golden petals of their hair closing around the withering florets of their faces.

A sadness had come with the single cloud. A feeling of realness which had always been connected to sadness because for Maria what was real was always sad. She couldn't live without the realness but she also couldn't live without its opposite. The sensations of possibility she felt throughout her body from the airport to the island had gone away and the happenings from the recent past (on the bus, on the train, on the ferry, and not so long ago on the bicycle) felt as if they happened in the distant past.

But the single cloud blocking the sun dissipated in all directions (while Maria wasn't looking)—when perhaps the unknown conditions she had always hoped would come to her aid, came to her aid for once—and the sunlight shimmered over and around her body and onto the face of the woman, who lifted her arm to shield her eyes from the brightness.

Maria felt the sensations of possibility again; felt that the happenings from the recent past (on the bus, on the train, on the ferry, and not so long ago on the bicycle)—and furthermore happenings from the distant past and the between-recent-and-distant past (picnicking with her mother in the Flower Viewing Garden, drawing the picture of the rowboat, practicing her slice forehand on the school's auditorium wall)—happened in the recent past and even more recently.

She turned to the sea, to look at what the children were pointing at but she had lost sight of the ferry and scanned the open waters to find it. She could see from one end of the 6 Cities to the other; the skyline of buildings; remembered the two women on the motorcycle; wondered where they were among the buildings; scanned the open waters again; saw the ferry; saw the children on the ferry—port, stern, starboard, and bow; saw them pointing in all directions.

see life

Something dark rose to the surface of the 6 Cities Sea—dilating like a pupil in the clear blue waters, surrounding the ferry. The children on board pointed in all directions as the darkness grew around them. Maria had seen only a small part of the darkness on her voyage to the island but from the perspective of distance and in full light, she saw it all. She didn't know how long she and the woman were going to be there, what they would do, or talk about. She left it to the next moment and the moment after that and so on. What would she do tomorrow with or without the woman? She would do something because there was always something to do until (and unless) she didn't want to do anything anymore.

But doing nothing required a decisiveness she never nurtured in herself though there was still time to do so. Doing nothing meant becoming nothing and becoming was only a matter of time and will. And yet she was relieved to wake up in the morning, to open her eyes and focus on the various objects in her room—the window curtains, the door knob, the light bulb—knowing she had beaten death for another day and that, with any luck (luck was all she needed), she would keep beating death until it finally won, when someone might say she fought the "good fight", that she lived a thousand lifetimes during her one little life, that she loved a little and was loved a little, and that her life was like a secret treasure buried beneath the sea—magnificent to behold were it not hidden away.

The woman stood up and brushed the grass and dirt from her elbows.

"What is it?" she asked Maria.

Maria pointed at the darkness floating up around the ferry and said (meant to say) "sea life" but whispered "see life" instead. The woman heard "sea life" and thought about dolphins. She walked over to Maria and stood beside her, didn't see—couldn't see—what Maria saw, but pretended to see it anyway.

--the end--

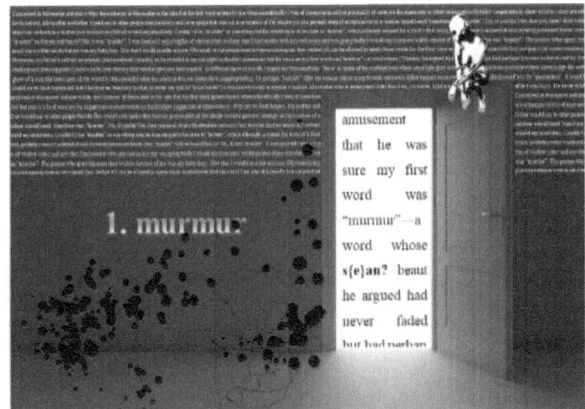

www.ingramcontent.com/pod-product-compliance
Lightning Source LLC
Chambersburg PA
CBHW030906170426
43193CB00009BA/756